animal attack!

SHARK ATTACKS

Patrick J. Fitzgerald

WITHDRAWN

HIGH
interest
books

Children's Press
A Division of Grolier Publishing
New York / London / Hong Kong / Sydney
Danbury, Connecticut

To my mother and father

Book Design: Kim M. Sonsky
Contributing Editor: Jennifer Ceaser and Claudia Isler

Photo Credits: p. 4 © The Everett Collection; pp. 6, 18, 38 Digital Stock; pp. 9, 25 © Amos Nachoum/Corbis; pp. 12–13 © Bill Curtsinger/National Geographic Society; p. 17 © Brandon C. Cole/Corbis; p. 27 © Charles O'Rear/Corbis; pp. 15, 29, 32 © Jeffrey L. Rottman/Corbis; p. 30 © Tom Brakefield/Corbis; p. 34 © Stuart Westmorland/Corbis.

Visit Children's Press on the Internet at:
http://publishing.grolier.com

Fitzgerald, Patrick, 1966-
    Shark attacks / by Patrick Fitzgerald.
        p. cm.—(Animal attacks)
    Includes bibliographical references (p.)
    Summary: Discusses the history of shark attacks on humans, the reasons why
        sharks attack, the importance of sharks to the world's oceans, and the need to
        save endangered species.
    ISBN 0-516-23318-1 (lib. bdg.)—ISBN 0-516-23518-4 (pbk.)
    1.   Shark attacks - Juvenile literature   [1. Shark
    attacks]   I. Title II. Series
        2000
597.3'15—dc21

contents

introduction

Say the words "shark attack," and most people think of the movie *Jaws*. In the 1975 film, a killer shark attacked people as they swam and played in the ocean. But the fear of being attacked by a shark is not something new. On the island of Fiji, in the Pacific Ocean, ceremonies were once held to make the ocean safe for fishing. Fishermen guided sharks into large nets. Then "shark-kissers" swam out, grabbed a shark, turned it over, and kissed its stomach. It was said that once a shark had been kissed, it would never attack a human being.

The poster for the 1975 movie *Jaws*

Introduction

Other cultures viewed sharks with both fear and respect. In ancient times, many island peoples worshipped sharks as gods. Hawaiian legends speak of the *mano-kanaka*. *Mano-kanaka* were sharks that took on the appearance of humans and then destroyed the land. It is said that islanders sacrificed humans to keep the shark gods happy.

In modern times, people are far more likely to kill a shark than to make friends with one. Each year, we kill about 100 million sharks. Some scientists say that we are overfishing sharks. This overfishing may be why shark attacks actually dropped worldwide in 1998.

Any shark can be dangerous. Yet there are only a few types of sharks that are considered to be true man-eaters. The two most well-known man-eating sharks are the great white and the tiger shark.

The great white shark is one of the world's most dangerous sharks.

chapter one

NATURAL-BORN PREDATORS

John Forse, an experienced surfer, will never forget a day in April 1998. He was catching some waves at Gleneden Beach, in Oregon. Forse was paddling on his surfboard when the ocean water began swirling in front of him. At first, Forse thought it was just a group of seals playing in the surf.

"The next thing I knew, I felt this pressure on my thigh," Forse told the Associated Press. "No pain—it was more like a vice grip." Forse said he didn't have time to be scared. He was just trying to survive. "The shark pulled me under about 12 feet (about 3 1/2 m)," Forse said from his hospital bed. He was recovering from a deep bite wound in his right thigh.

He had been attacked by a 15-foot (4 ¹/₂-m) great white, the deadliest of all the oceans' sharks.

How did the surfer manage to escape? "I knew that sharks had a sensitive spot on their nose but I couldn't reach it," Forse explained. "His dorsal (back) fin was about a foot away, so I started beating on it."

Forse then climbed back on his board, which had a 12-inch (30-cm) bite taken out of it. He was able to paddle back to shore, despite his injury. The entire attack lasted for only twenty seconds. Forse was taken to the hospital, where his wound was treated. He plans to go surfing again as soon as he can.

Forse's survival of the great white attack is common. In fact, most shark attacks are not fatal. So if a shark doesn't want to eat you, what makes a shark attack?

WHY SHARKS ATTACK

Sharks first appeared on Earth nearly 400 million years ago. They are one of the world's oldest and most dangerous predators. Yet sharks are also shy creatures that will usually avoid people. In fact, most shark attacks are believed to be cases of mistaken identity. Sharks may mistake surfers, divers, snorkelers, and swimmers for their regular food. People who dive, snorkel, surf, or swim make splashing and kicking movements similar to those of fish and seals. Fish and seals are two of the shark's favorite meals.

Sharks also are attracted to blood. If there are cuts on a swimmer's or diver's body, the blood will attract the shark. Also, many fishermen will keep fish that they catch close to them. A shark, attracted to the bleeding fish, may mistake a fisherman for shark food.

Sharks are very sensitive to electrical fields, or areas, in the water. Fish and other animals in the ocean produce electrical charges that create these fields. A shark uses these fields to detect movement and locate its prey. Metal objects create electrical charges similar to those produced by a

shark's normal prey. Thus, a shark may mistaken-
ly attack a human who is wearing something made
of metal, such as a watch or jewelry.

Sharks also will attack anything that has invad-
ed their territory. A territory is an area that is

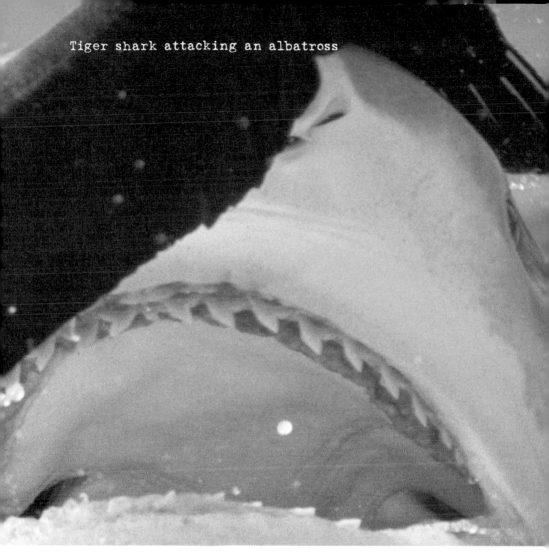

occupied and defended by an animal. Swimmers, divers, and snorkelers may unknowingly trespass on a shark's territory. The shark will use signals to tell the intruder that it feels threatened. Sharks will twist their bodies, arch their backs, and shake their heads in warning. Most people do not recognize these signals, however, and risk being attacked.

Surfers are the people most likely to be attacked by sharks. According to researchers at the University of Florida, surfers make up 69 percent of shark-attack victims worldwide. Divers, fishermen, snorkelers, and swimmers make up most of the remaining 31 percent.

Fortunately, sharks are said not to like the taste of humans. That is why they usually attack only once. The shark will realize its mistake and swim away. To a shark, a wet suit-covered surfer is not as tasty as a fat, blubbery seal.

NUMBER OF ATTACKS

Sharks do attack people, but not as often as we might think. Worldwide, there are only about one hundred shark attacks on people each year. Between ten and fifteen people die as a result of these attacks. Compared with the number of

Shark attack wounds (large picture), and the same wounds after surgery (small picture).

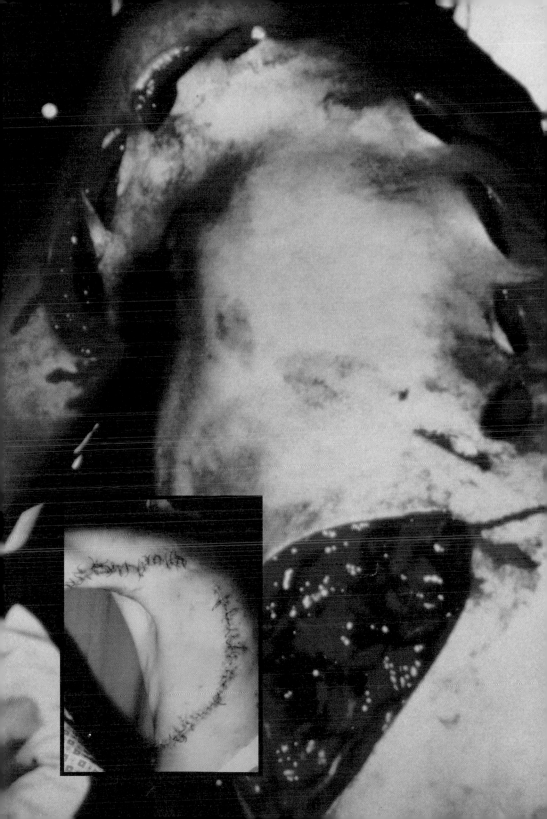

did you know?

Sharks will sink if they stop swimming. This means that a shark cannot swim backward or come to a sudden stop.

people killed by sharks, almost fifty times as many people die by drowning each year. Bees, snakes, and dogs are responsible for many more deaths each year than are sharks. In fact, a person is thirty times more likely to be hit by lightning than be killed by a shark.

ABOUT THE SHARK

Sharks are fish. However, sharks differ from most fish in that their skeletons are made of cartilage, not bone. But, as other fish do, sharks breathe through their gills. They must swim constantly to breathe. Sharks swim through the water by moving their tail fins. The tail fin helps them to change direction. To move up or down, they use their pectoral, or side, fins.

Sharks' nostrils are used only to smell, not to breathe.

Sharks have excellent eyesight, hearing, and sense of smell. Using its hearing, a shark can sense when a sea animal is in trouble. Then it goes after the animal because it is easier to capture. Shark nostrils are only used for smelling and not for breathing. The great white's nostrils can smell one drop of blood in 25 gallons (95 liters) of water. Sharks also can sense electrical charges in other animals. This sense means that they can notice the smallest movements around them. They use these electrical charges to locate their prey.

chapter two

GREAT WHITE SHARKS

On October 5, 1996, at Dillon Beach, California, Joey Hanlon was attacked by an 18-foot (6-m) great white. Hanlon was 100 yards (91 m) from shore, in 10 feet (3 m) of water, when the attack occurred.

Hanlon said he "felt a nudge." He then felt a horrible pain shoot through his leg. He looked down and saw the huge jaws and teeth of a great white. The shark flipped over Hanlon and his surfboard. Then it clamped onto Hanlon's torso, tearing into his stomach. Passengers on a nearby boat saw the attack. They quickly piloted the boat to the injured surfer. As the rescuers pulled Hanlon onto the deck of the boat,

The great white shark is the world's largest meat-eating fish.

his intestines spilled out of his wet suit. A medic on board the boat gently pushed them back into his body.

After four hours of surgery, the doctors were able to save Hanlon. It took more than 350 stitches to put him back together.

Great whites account for one-half to one-third of the approximately one hundred shark attacks each year. Of these thirty to fifty great white attacks, only ten to fifteen are fatal.

JAWS!

Of the 350 known species of sharks, the great white shark is probably the most famous. It was certainly the biggest star of the movie *Jaws!* The great white is not the largest shark in the world—the whale shark and basking shark are larger—but it is the most dangerous. The largest great white ever caught was 29 feet (9 m) long and weighed more than 7,000 pounds (3,150 kg). It is the largest carnivorous (meat-eating) fish on Earth. Great whites usually live alone but sometimes do travel in pairs. They never travel in groups. They also never stop growing.

The great white is named for its large size and white belly. Great whites have narrow, triangle-shaped teeth that look like a saw blade. Their bottom teeth are used to grab and hold prey. Their rough-edged front teeth are used for cutting. Behind the front row lie many more rows of teeth.

A great white has several rows of razor-sharp teeth.

Each tooth is ready to pop into place when the one in front of it is lost. At any one time, a great white has 3,000 teeth in its mouth. It is said that a great white may go through 20,000 teeth in a lifetime!

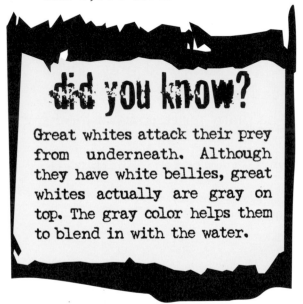

did you know?

Great whites attack their prey from underneath. Although they have white bellies, great whites actually are gray on top. The gray color helps them to blend in with the water.

WHERE THEY LIVE

Great whites are found in all the world's oceans. They live in both warm tropical waters and cold polar seas. In the United States, they can be found along the West Coast, East Coast, and most of the Gulf Coast. Great whites also can be found in the waters of Australia, the eastern coastline of China, Japan, the Mediterranean Sea, southern Russia,

Scandinavia, South Africa, South America, and West Africa. Great whites normally live in very deep water. However, they may swim into shallow water to find food. As they get into shallower water, they come into greater contact with people. Most great white attacks occur in the Pacific Ocean off the coasts of the United States and Australia. There are many surfers, divers, and snorkelers in these areas. Many attacks also take place in the Atlantic and Indian oceans off the coast of South Africa.

WHAT THEY EAT

Great whites eat a variety of ocean animals. Adult great whites prefer large sea mammals, such as seals and sea lions. They also will eat other sharks and carrion (animals that are already dead). Young great whites, which have narrower teeth than the adults do, eat mostly fish. A great white can stock up on food and go without eating for up to three months.

HOW THEY HUNT

The great white is the only shark—the only fish—that can poke its head out of the water. No one knows exactly why it does this. One theory is that the shark is able to spot seals and sea lions as they dive into the water.

A great white attacks by taking its prey by surprise. It can swim up to 15 miles (24 km) per hour. The great white raises its snout (the front part of its head), drops its lower jaw, and shoves its upper jaw forward. Then it moves the lower jaw upward and forward to bite its prey. The shark's jaws are so strong that it can separate a leg or an arm from a person's body in just one bite. The great white doesn't chew its food. Instead, it tears off pieces of its prey and swallows them whole. A great white can eat a human in a matter of minutes.

As with other sharks, the great white will roll its eyeballs back in its head when attacking. This action protects the shark's eyes from being harmed by its struggling prey.

A great white is the only type of shark that can poke its head out of the water.

chapter three

TIGER SHARKS

On July 30, 1945, two torpedoes hit the war ship USS *Indianapolis. The ship sank in just twelve minutes off the island of Pelieu in the South Pacific. Many of the crew died instantly. The corpses and body parts of dead sailors slowly sank into the ocean. The surviving sailors bobbed up and down on flotation devices, waiting to be rescued. But before the U.S. Navy could reach the men, the tiger sharks did.*

The shark attacks began at sunrise the first day after the ship went down. The tiger sharks were probably first attracted by the bloody corpses of the dead sailors. Sailor Woody James was floating

The tiger shark is smaller than the great white, but it can be just as deadly.

in the water with a group of about 150 men when the sharks arrived.

"The day wore on and the sharks were around," recalled James. *"You'd hear guys scream, especially in the afternoon. It seemed like the sharks were worse in the afternoon than during the days."*

The tiger sharks used bump-and-bite attacks to pick off men who were at the edge of the group. They would circle a sailor and then bump him before biting him several times. This is normal feeding behavior for tiger sharks.

Of the 900 men who made it through the explosion, only 317 were alive when rescuers arrived five days later. Tiger sharks had killed and eaten almost all of the rest.

JAWS, TOO!

The tiger shark is one of the most feared sharks in the world. The tiger shark gets its name from the dark stripes across its body. These stripes fade as the shark grows older. Along with the great white

The sand tiger shark

and the bull shark, it is one of the three deadliest species of shark. It is known to attack boats and eat humans on a regular basis. Most shark victims of air and sea disasters are killed by tiger sharks.

The average tiger shark is between 10 and 15 feet (3-4 $^1/_2$ m) long and weighs about 1,110 pounds (500 kg). The largest can grow to 25 feet (7 $^1/_2$ m) and weigh more than 2,220 pounds (1,000 kg).

The tiger shark prefers to live in warm seas.

WHERE THEY LIVE

Unlike the great white, which can live in colder waters, the tiger shark only lives in warm bodies of water. It travels alone in warm seas all over the world. During the winter months, tiger sharks often swim near the equator, where the water is extremely warm. Each year, a tiger shark may swim up to 1,500 miles (2,500 km) to migrate, or move to warmer areas. In the summer, tiger sharks can be found off the coasts of New York and Southern California. They also may live in the salty water of certain lagoons and rivers. The tiger shark will swim up to 50 miles (80 km) a day to reach its destination.

HOW THEY HUNT

Tiger sharks have good eyesight, but they use their excellent sense of smell to locate prey. In fact, almost two-thirds of a tiger shark's brain is used just for processing information related to smell. As with the great white, the tiger shark can pick up the scent of even the tiniest trace of blood. Tiger sharks are also very sensitive to movement. They can tell when a fish or sea animal is wounded simply by the way it moves. Wounded prey are easier to catch.

The tiger shark is built to be a deadly predator. With its long tail, it can reach speeds of more than 20 miles (32 km) per hour. It has a wedge-shaped head, a large mouth, and powerful jaws.

A baby shark is called a pup. Tiger sharks can give birth to up to eighty-two pups at a time!

Its teeth are razor-sharp, allowing the shark to chomp through even the toughest sea turtle shell. The first two rows of teeth are used to catch prey. The remaining rows of teeth are replacement teeth. A new tooth will rotate into place once an old tooth is lost or broken.

WHAT THEY EAT

The tiger shark has no real special food that it likes. In fact, it is known as the "garbage" shark because it will eat anything in sight. Shoes, dogs, license plates, deer antlers, crocodiles' heads, even an entire suit of armor—they've all been found in the stomachs of tiger sharks.

chapter four

THE FUTURE OF SHARKS

Ray McAllister is a professor of ocean engineering in Florida. In early 1990, McAllister and his friend joined a small guided tour to sail off the coast of Panama. McAllister recalls the terrifying moments of a great white attack.

"While [we were] eating lunch, the bow (front) of the boat reared up and started to shake," McAllister told the Associated Press. His friend was at the boat's controls, holding onto another man who was sliding back to the rear of the boat.

The men turned around and realized that they were staring at the head of a giant white shark. *"The shark had the entire rear of the boat and two*

did you know?

Each year, humans kill millions of sharks. Sharks kill fewer than fifty people annually.

engines in its mouth," McAllister continued. "The guide had his hands on the shark's nose to keep from sliding backwards." The guide pushed off from the shark's nose and grabbed the boat's controls. With one hand, he turned on the engines and threw them into gear.

Great clouds of shark meat, cartilage, teeth, and blood shot all over the men, the boat, and the water. They watched as the dark ocean swallowed up the bloody carcass of the great white shark.

This incident is one of many in recent years that have involved sharks and boats. Contact between humans and sharks is on the rise in many parts of the world. One reason for this increase is that more people have moved to coastal areas. As a result, the number of people using the water for swimming and other kinds of recreation is growing. These are the same waters where sharks swim and look for food.

SHARK HUNTING

Although sharks may pose a threat to humans, humans are far more dangerous to sharks. The number of sharks, especially great whites, has decreased in recent years. This decline is because of years of being hunted by humans. In many cases, sharks are hunted only for their fins. In some countries, shark fins are thought to give people special powers.

Sharks also are almost disease-free. For this reason, some people who are looking for protection from disease eat shark meat. However, scientists have determined that the shark's resistance to disease can't be transferred to humans.

PROTECTING SHARKS

Of the 350 types of sharks, eighty species are in danger of becoming extinct. A species that is

Without sharks, our oceans would become very sick.

extinct no longer exists. Sharks are very much at risk of extinction because they reproduce and grow so slowly.

Only recently have people become concerned about killing and overfishing sharks. That's partly because humans are just beginning to understand these fish and how important they are to the world's oceans. Sharks are apex predators, meaning that they are at the top of the food chain. Without sharks, our oceans would become very sick. Sharks control fish and sea animal populations. Otherwise,

The Future of Sharks

these populations would become too large, throwing the ocean's food chain out of balance.

Some countries are beginning to recognize that many species of sharks are endangered. Australia, California, and South Africa have given great whites protected status as a species. In the United States, the National Marine Fisheries Service has reduced the number of sharks that can be killed each year.

Unfortunately, sharks don't recognize international borders. Even if they're protected in some countries, as soon as they enter the waters of a country where their fins or meat are wanted, they're out of luck.

As scientists learn more about sharks, it becomes clear that the world's oceans need sharks to remain healthy. Experts hope that more countries will try to protect them. Although sharks can be dangerous, in time we may be able to look at this fascinating creature and see more than just its jaws.

FACT SHEET

There are 350 species of sharks in the world. These include the blue shark, the dogfish shark, the mako shark, the nurse shark, and the whale shark.

Great white shark

Carcharodon carcharias The scientific (Latin) name for the great white shark.
Size: averaging 12-16 feet (3.7-4.9 m), weighing about 7,000 pounds (3200 kg)
Habitat: most of the world's temperate (not too hot or too cold) oceans

Tiger shark

Galeocerdo cuvier The scientific (Latin) name for the tiger shark.
Size: averaging 10-20 feet (3-6 m), weighing about 1,000 pounds (450 kg)
Habitat: tropical seas and some temperate seas worldwide

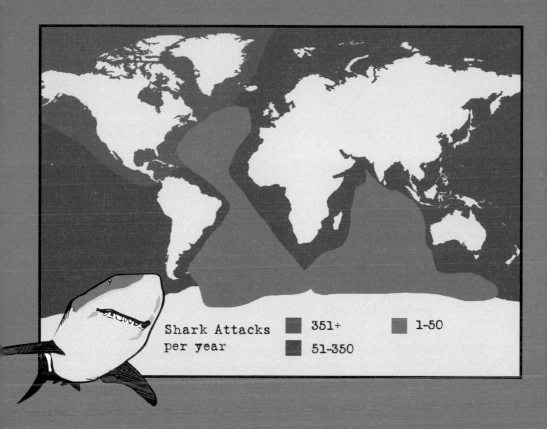

Shark Attacks per year

- 351+
- 51-350
- 1-50

Life Span

No one is certain what the life span is for the great white or the tiger shark. Some experts estimate that the great white can live for up to 100 years. A tiger shark is thought to live for thirty to forty years.

bull shark one of the three most dangerous types of man-eating sharks

bump-and-bite a type of shark attack in which the shark bumps the victim before attacking

carcass a dead body

carnivorous meat-eating

carrion an animal that is already dead

cartilage flexible body part that makes up a shark's skeleton, instead of bone

conservation the careful protection of animals

dorsal fin a fin on the back or top of a fish

endangered threatened with becoming extinct

extinct a species that no longer exists

gills part of a fish's body that lets it take oxygen from water so that it can breathe

great white the most dangerous species of shark

habitat an area where an animal naturally lives and grows

mammals warm-blooded animals

mano-kanaka legendary Hawaiian gods who were half man, half shark

migrate to move to warmer areas

mistaken identity type of shark attack in which a shark mistakes a person for its regular prey

pectoral fins fins on the side of a shark's body; they are used to help it change direction

predator an animal that hunts and kills other animals

prey an animal that is killed and eaten for food

pup a baby shark

snout the front part of the head of an animal

species a group of animals belonging to the same classification of animal

territory an area that is occupied and defended by an animal or group of animals

tiger shark the second most dangerous man-eating shark

wet suit rubber suit worn by divers and surfers to keep them warm

resources

American Zoo and Aquarium Association
P.O. Box 79863
Baltimore, MD 21279
Web site: *www.aza.org*
Has links to local national zoos and aquariums and tells what each organization is doing to save endangered species. Also has information about AZA programs and how you can become involved, research links, and a photo gallery.

Center for Marine Conservation
1725 DeSales Street, NW
Washington, DC 20036
Phone: 202/429-5609
Web site: *www.cmc-ocean.org*
Outlines ways to protect oceans and marine life. Contains a searchable library, information about conservation programs, activities (including experiments), and general data about ocean life.

Florida Museum of Natural History's Shark Page
www.flmnh.ufl.edu/fish/sharks/sharks.htm
General information about the kinds of sharks and how, when, why, and where they attack. Includes updated shark news from around the world and provides links to other shark sites and shark conservation organizations.

The Center for Shark Research
www.mote.org/~rhueter/sharks/shark.phtml
Get information about shark characteristics, behavior, diseases, myths, and attacks. The site describes different shark research programs and how you can get involved in shark conservation.

for further reading

Ambrose, Greg. *Shark Bites: True Stories of Survival.* Honolulu: Bess Press, Inc., 1996.

MacCormick, Alex. *Shark Attacks.* New York: Tor Books, 1998.

Matthiessen, Peter. *Blue Meridian: The Search for the Great White Shark.* New York: Viking Penguin, 1997.

Murray, Kirsty. *Man-Eaters and Bloodsuckers.* New South Wales, Australia: Allen & Unwin, 1998.

index

ABOUT THE AUTHOR

Patrick J. Fitzgerald is a freelance writer who has had a lifelong interest in sharks. He lives in Brooklyn, NY, with his wife Wendy, two cats, and a dog.